Another Troy

poems by
Joan Wehlen Morrison

edited by
Susan Signe Morrison

Finishing Line Press
Georgetown, Kentucky

Another Troy

To Jim, Sarah, and John for their wise advice and deepest thanks to Beverly Smith for her generous love

Copyright © 2020 by Susan Signe Morrison
ISBN 978-1-64662-258-0 First Edition
All rights reserved under International and Pan-American Copyright Conventions. No part of this book may be reproduced in any manner whatsoever without written permission from the publisher, except in the case of brief quotations embodied in critical articles and reviews.

ACKNOWLEDGMENTS

Prior Work for Joan Wehlen Morrison:
American Mosaic: The Immigrant Experience in the Words of Those Who Lived It
From Camelot to Kent State: The Sixties Experience in the Words of Those Who Lived It
Home Front Girl: A Diary of Love, Literature, and Growing Up in Wartime America

Prior Work for Susan Signe Morrison:
Women Pilgrims in Late Medieval England: Private Piety as Public Performance
Excrement in the Late Middle Ages: Sacred Filth and Chaucer's Fecopoetics
The Literature of Waste: Material Ecopoetics and Ethical Matter
A Medieval Woman's Companion: Women's Lives in the European Middle Ages
Grendel's Mother: The Saga of the Wyrd-Wife
Editor of *Home Front Girl: A Diary of Love, Literature, and Growing Up in Wartime America*

Funded in part by Finishing Line Press' One Last Word Program.

Publisher: Leah Maines
FLP Editor: Christen Kincaid
Cover Art: Joan Wehlen Morrison in 1943, age 20
Author Photo: Jim Kilfoyle
Cover Design: Elizabeth Maines McCleavy

Order online: www.finishinglinepress.com
also available on amazon.com

Author inquiries and mail orders:
Finishing Line Press
P. O. Box 1626
Georgetown, Kentucky 40324
U. S. A.

Table of Contents

I Dreamt I Dwelt 1
Possession 2
On the War-Dead: For Armistice 3
Sanctum Sanctorum 4
Karnak Is Dead 5
Metaphor 6
Puck 7
Nature Hut 8
New York World's Fair 1939 9
I Bumped into a Star 10
For a Moment 11
Did I Make the World? 12
In Memory of August 31, 1939 13
On Reading Virgil, Book IV, Lines 375-419 14
Joan Wehlen 15
A.D. 79 16
The Writer 17
Now in this April 18
God, Kiss the World Tonight 19
To a Fallen German 20
Cassandra 1940 21
Reminiscence of Days Gone Now 22
Last Year Before War Came 23
Holiness 24
In Memoriam November 28 25
H. 27
Paris 28
Remembered from Easter 29
The Storm 30
The Moon Is a Bent Feather 31
House Cleaning 32
Now It Is Come 33
Pledge 34
Once 35
If There Were No More World 37

Foreward by Susan Signe Morrison

After the death of my mother, Joan Wehlen Morrison, my brothers and I found her diaries, notebooks, and poetry from the 1930s and 1940s. The diaries describe her life in the city of Chicago—from pining for handsome boys in ROTC uniforms to her love for the Art Institute, Lake Michigan and, later, campus life at the University of Chicago. She ruminates about daily headlines and major touchstones of the era: the Lindbergh kidnapping, FDR on the radio, *Goodbye Mr. Chips* and *Citizen Kane*, Garbo, Churchill, Hitler, war work, and Red Cross meetings. An edited volume of her diaries, *Home Front Girl: A Diary of Love, Literature, and Growing Up in Wartime America*, has been called "better than fiction."

While some of Joan's childhood poems have topics like a Jack O'Lantern, Jackie Frost, or Santa Claus, in November 1932 in the midst of the Great Depression she writes at age nine, 'Cheer Up!' "This country, it's got to cheer up, and why not today?/ So cheer up, cheer up, for the U.S.A./ This depression, it's got to break up....So! Come on, cheer up!/ Don't be a snob,/ Go find a job:/ Today!" Her socialist political leanings emerge when she pens 'The Saga of Eric the Red.' In honor of a Viking explorer who travelled to the New World, it begins with this bold stanza: "Eric was a communist/ Eric was a red/ He told his employers/ He wished they were dead."

Inspired to write verse in the vein of Robert Louis Stevenson and Lewis Carroll, poetry was woven into her diary entries. Emoting "Thank Heaven for Kipling!", Joan wryly observes at age fourteen, "That shows what reading Kipling can do—it's made me a better Englishman than American." Other favorites include A. E. Housman and John Donne. At age fifteen, she encounters *As You Like It*. "Shakespeare makes the awfullest puns—worse than Jack Benny—really!" Working at a biscuit factory for the military in summer 1941, Joan is so bored she recites poetry to herself. "Have gone through Housman—Shakespeare—all the speeches from *Julius Caesar* and everything I like . . . the sonnets."

The poetry in this volume, written from age fifteen to her early twenties, tells a unique—and true—story as she loses her innocence due to the impending war and its violent arrival and as she comes of age as a poet and writer. While the title of this volume, *Another Troy*, comes from Joan's passion for classical literature, she remains a girl. Despite her ability to see deeply into things, she makes fun of herself at age fifteen: "Well, had to translate eight lines of Latin poetry for Humanities tonight. Very gloomy—all about 'death conquers everything—the mountains fall over and nothing is left for a long time'—boo hoo." Classical literature gives her sustenance. In April 1941, she listens to the news, pondering what will happen if England is invaded, a not unlikely possibility at the time: "Maybe England shall go down. I was thinking of Cicero today as we heard Churchill. And how those brave words would sound when some schoolboy is translating them, a thousand years hence. Maybe England shall fall. I guess so. I don't know." Yet Joan never lost her ability to feel compassion, even for the so-called enemy.

I hope you will enjoy these poems, sent, as it were, in a time capsule to our moment today. They remind us how the written word remains a means for hope for those in emotional extremity—from passionate love to dire political circumstances—both in terms of what one can read and what one can write.

I Dreamt I Dwelt
(January 14, 1938)

I dreamt I dwelt beside green fields
  Where all the brooks ran gold
Where sky was blue and loud the wind
  And man did not grow old.

I dreamt that dreams were not in vain
  That laughs were ever new,
I dreamt those things last night, my dear,
  Because I dreamt of you.

Possession
(September 9, 1938)

These things are mine:
    Days that I have known when the
    wind was like a boy's breath.
    And evenings when the clouds
    were purple over the trees.
    Nights when the insects were
    singing to the young thin moon.
No one can take these from me,
    They are signed over to me by Time.
    He has deeded them to me; because
    I knew these things once,
    they are mine forever.
These also are mine:
    The tree that stands lonely and
    grey against the lake.
    Red and green salt cellars on
    a yellow cloth in the sun.
    Your face when you are laughing
    with the rain on your cheeks.
Because I have known them, they are mine forever.
    And my own life is mine to live over
    if so I will it; because I was,
    I can always be young.
So these are mine:
    the first day of the circus with
    the elephants and peanuts
    a glamour in my head;
The time I saw the whole,
    gigantic curve of everything;
    The first time I saw your face
    with your eyes like flaming hollows.
So all these things are mine.
    They say: in experiencing, we kill
    experience. True, but the
    memory lingers on. And we
    can dream forever.

If it is all a dream, I want to dream
    Always of you.

On the War-Dead: For Armistice
    (November 7, 1938)

I saw your name in the list today.
    You were a nice boy; I remember you.
You used to sit behind me in Geometry
And hum Wagner softly during the theorems.
No one else heard you, but I did.
Perhaps that is why I did not understand Geometry.
You were always humming Wagner
Softly—ever so softly to the Evening Star during theorems.
    You were a nice boy; I remember you.
You had curly blonde hair and we used to make up funny poems
About each other and the rest of the world.
I remember you. We used to argue, too,
Remember (I forget—you remember no more)
About rearmament and the Road to Peace.
That's funny—the Road to Peace—and you dead out there.
    You were a nice boy; I remember you.
You didn't mean anything to me. I had forgotten
You til today when I saw your name in the list.
You came back to me like a wind from the old schoolroom.
You were going to be president—to see your name in print.
Ah—! It is in print now—in the list of those killed.
But you do not see it. I wish I hadn't. And there are others
    In the list, all nice boys, and someone
        Remembers them all.

Sanctum Sanctorum
    (February 22, 1939)

There is one holy place
They cannot desecrate,
The holy place
Given into my keeping,
Wholly encirclèd
Within me,
The holy temple
Of my body.
And far within the wall of flesh
Lying guarded sleeps
The holy of holies
The inviolate, the fastidious
The secret chamber of my soul,
Wherein there is
An altar raised
To immortality.

Karnak Is Dead
    (February 24, 1939)

Karnak is dead
And Thebes is fallen
Holy Ilios has long lain low.

Arthur of the flowing beard
Tristan with the silvered helm
Cleopatra, green-shadowed queen,
Nefertiti in her cool white tomb,
Alexander for all the worlds he saw
At last was held in a small cold urn,
No more echoes from Roland's horn, and Siegfried,
Who first touched the bitter taste of dawn—
Dreaming names all that held the wine of life.
Where are they now? Ashes and mold.

And at best you can say,
"Here is the cup she drank of."
But where is the red-white cup of Helen's body
That once held all the joy of life?
Fallen columns
Broken idols and forgotten Gods
Are all that remain in Karnak;
Turned to grey dust
And whitened bone
        Is Helen.

Metaphor
    (June 17, 1939)

I am a moving window
Through which colors and form pass
But which
    Holds nothing.

Puck
      (June 24, 1939)

Puck, are you dead
Or am I dead
Or is this thing within me dead?

If I cannot find
Him far outside,
Perhaps he is hiding—within.

Here, Puck.
No, I guess I am too old
Or I have forgotten how.

Stamp on the new grass
Three times and wish.
Where are you, Puck?

I guess I must be silly
Believing in faeries,
A big girl like me.

I don't believe there are any.
There, now you must come;
I have challenged you.

But, still: the flapping of wings.

Nature Hut
    (August 18, 1939)

I have my prairie broken window
that looks out to nowhere.
Sometimes I look through it and
a feeling of isolation, of wind around the corner,
comes to me and I feel utterly alone
in my little green and white house—
the prairie wind coming
through the thin fringe of trees
and the broken window to me.

New York World's Fair 1939
(September 4, 1939, three days after the Germans invade Poland)

We shall remember this peace—
This caught moment of half-night beauty.
Music—and a night bird blinded by the spotlight,
That same light which has just flashed,
Following it as it moves on a white cloud.
Music—the last rose of summer chimes so sweet,
I am afraid I shall have to forget it
Or die, not hearing it again.
The pylon gleams and the sphere is pale blue in the night.
White shall be this memory forever, I think.
The last rose of summer is too beautiful, I fear.
Even the wind is white.

Some day they shall dig up this circle,
Row upon stone row of seats—
And the molded screen and the broken figure
Atop this tower will be half-gone—or all
And the lights ungleaming
But they shall know we passed.
They will wonder, perhaps, who sat here,
What motley crowd idled—it is we here
In our colorful rest that they shall wonder of.
The red flag flying and the stalwart figure atop
      May still remain in tatters.

But I—this girl in the blue dress and Juliet cap—
I will be utterly disappeared.
Uncurled from the stone seat and unlistening then
To any music—even this last rose chiming.
Even then, though, even then when they ponder these ruins
And this place is ivy-grown and moss,
Even then, though,
I think we shall remember this peace.

I Bumped into a Star
(September 10, 1939)

I bumped into a star once
        I didn't know it would give me
        Such an electric shock
        But I am still tingling from it
        All the little bright points of light still prick me.
        Oh, I am drunken with stars.
        I must go and bump into another someday.

For a Moment
    (September 23, 1939)

For a moment
The world stood still
The needle on the phonograph
Forgot to move
And the waterfall outside
Froze still.
The world, for a moment,
Ceased to turn.

Then you spoke.

Did I Make the World?
(September 25, 1939)

Here are we two and the night is white clouded
And the dream-music drifting out the window
Punctuated at the hour by themes broadcast
And we return to *Träumerei*.
I can hardly believe
Even now the pulp of flesh is draining white
In Poland, that there is any life anywhere
Save this dream life of ours.
Perhaps all this world is only 'I imagine.'
All mine. I made it.

In Memory of August 31, 1939
(September 27, 1939)

I remember standing in the crooked shadow of the Catalpa tree
The August-September night it started.
White moon on the grass and moon mist over the fields.
Even then. It was so still. How could we know?
The crickets sang farewell to summer.
And the smell of a golden reaping
Was rich in the air. How could we know?
Even then, while we were so still,
Somewhere the guns were beginning to boom
And another crop was being harvested.

On Reading Virgil, Book IV, Lines 375-419
(November 20, 1939)

Old words, old thoughts, old phrases,
New lips, new mouths, new tongues.
How long has life thus returned?
How long still returning she?
But now only for a little while
The ancient words pass through my mouth.

Dido, who never lived,
Is so much much more immortal
Than I,
So enormously present today
Who dies tomorrow.
She, Dido, who never lived,
Will wake men's hearts a thousand years from now.

Joan Wehlen
(February 21, 1940)

In my name is Weland the god
And in faint blue lines beneath my wrist
Is running the pulse of two peoples.

I may not lightly treat myself.
I am more valuable than marble
Streaked with blue lines,
I am myself—a human being, particular.

A.D. 79
(February 25, 1940)

It was the end of summer and the sun
Was sending shafts of light upon Pompeii.
Dust drifted through the pillars dull with heat
And merchants hawked their wares in dulcet tones:
Grain from Odessa and marble from Paros
Silver from Ephesus and a headless god from Crete.
A dog snapped at a fly and a woman called a child.
The air is thick with peace and city-noise,
The bay is a blue jewel on the earth.
A boat has docked from Greece and the small boys
Are gathered round to see what it has brought.
The men sing as they carry coloured burdens from the East—
A vase from Knossos and a statuette from Thebes,
The arms of the slaves gleaming as they move.
One of the boys asks, "Where is Troy?" The men laugh.
A heaviness of heat lies soundless on the air.
Inside a window two are reading in the sun:
The boy slowly: "Non omnis moriar."
The man nods, the sunlight through the walls is thick with gold.
When evening comes, they listless sup with heat.

And when the roar begins, they shrug at first
And laugh, "The gods are mad tonight,"
The gods they never quite believed upon.
And the curtain of eternity fell on a stage
With smothering blackness—and death.

Against the crooked trees of that bizarre night, a wind flared.
A girl ran through the street, her cape flapping, scared.
A noise of query rose, then fright and then despair,
A mad race for the sea now black with wind,
Then captured by the ashes of hot death
And all the businessmen and little boys were dead.

I can stand the broken gods of Troy all lost
Or all the empty temples by the sea of Greece
Poets and the philosophers of ancient worlds all dead—

But not the loaves of bread at Pompeii
        ....still uneaten.

The Writer
(March 16, 1940)

The only thing I ever wrote
That will outlast my life is this:
My name in the wet cement of an old sidewalk.
Now it is dry and hard and faintly blurred
But still the letters I can trace
That spell my life.

And all the soul-words that I ever traced
On paper will have perished when I die
Or long before. But this—
The childish scrawl of a once-groping hand—
Will stay. Years after, people passing
Will kick at the cracked sidewalk
Wondering whose was the hand that vainly wrote in it,
And, in a while, earth will erase the work I made
And a new sidewalk will be laid or a new city built
And then, surely, I shall have gained
Annihilation.

Now in this April
  (April 7, 1940)

Now in this April of our dying
God grant us beauty
For we have desperate need of her.
Here in the throbbing heart of life
Caught in motion, mad with noise
We have the dying need
Of seeing beauty,
Thus receiving unction and absolution
For having lived.

God, Kiss the World Tonight
(May 26, 1940, day of prayer in England for the troops in Dunkirk)

God, kiss the world tonight
It is in sore need of caressing
Because we hate—
And most of all
Because there is an empty orchard in Flanders
Rotting in the rain
While the apple blossoms fall.

To a Fallen German
   (June 9, 1940, the day the Norwegian government falls to Germany)

Oh you—you are just a number
In our "Hundreds of Enemy Gloriously Slain,"
An enemy dead somewhere in the mud—
But I can see you as a little boy
Blonde and chasing butterflies and eating jam
A long time ago like all my brothers.
I think I would have liked you.

I cannot give you any word and all eternity
Is a veil between us. But soldier,
If there is an afterworld,
I wish you luck
And if not
You have no longer any need of it.

And I shall be with you soon.

Cassandra 1940
    (August 6, 1940)

I can see your name
On the white list of those who died
In some not distant future
That seems already past
After seeing your name
On the list of war-dead.
I take out an old photograph
Of a boy with a mandolin in the sun
And look at it with quickened memory
Of the face long forgotten
And then
Look at the list again.

I see it all quite clearly
It is already done.

Reminiscence of Days Gone Now
(August 1, 1940)

We never thought last year, when we
lay in summer comfort on the grass or
parted in idle walk the shimmering
corn fields or listened through the
long afternoons to the hum of the locusts,
that next year this time Paris would
be fallen, France subdued. We were
alive to nature then—war was
a drummery dream somewhere over
the green hills—as it is now too—
Even this year we do not believe
war, but such a change from
one summer to the next—who
knows where we shall be
next year this time?

Last Year Before War Came
(August 6, 1940)

Last year before war came
there still was a half-hope
war would not come.

And now
all the brave words are rotten
and we know we were fools to believe them
and I know
the words are rotten
and illusions
lie.

Holiness
(November 13, 1940)

Funny
How things change
As we age.
God isn't so holy
But the funny ways of the little boy
Next door
Who was a soldier and died
Suddenly are.

In Memoriam November 28
(January 16, 1941)

She looked out the window
and watched the soft powdery snow
settle on the cracks
in the grey stone.
The sky was white
and against it
the bare trees stood out
like black lace.
The warm sizzle of the radiator
and the beyond-consciousness feel
of its heat penetrated an inch
through her body.
The smell of wet clothes drying
was sweet and pungent in her nose
and a far off monotone was reading
from *Fra Lippo Lippi,*
'What is beauty?'
Over and beyond
all these senses there was
another sense of being.
She was reliving the just lived past,
the moment of meeting again the beloved.
The way he looked,
the way she looked,
what he said,
his eyes.
A tingle went through her
as she thought of it.

Miss Campbell was droning on.
This is life,
the present cannot come again.
The snow is falling
as in a paperweight.
Turn world,
burn world,
night is falling.

She raised her hand
and with another part of her

recited brilliantly
on the theme
of *Fra Lippo Lippi*.

H.
      (February 28, 1941)

Platonism, is, I guess, all right
And I still subscribe to it.
But darling, what I want right now
Is something Epicurean,
Immensely so.
Something intimately connected with
The touch of your smooth red lips.
Though through all this
I still can feel, I know
In any sort of action, any love—
We two would be
Both passionless
And somehow separated by a wall of space
That liking could not pierce
Nor contact break.
We are both reserved from each other—
But darling, platonic as I know we are,
I fear, against all reason, I still want to be
Immensely Epicurean with you.

Paris
> *(April 17, 1941)*

Paris must have fallen on a night like this,
All honey-fresh scented and sleepy.
I felt her breathe just now.
Troy must have fallen too, in spring.

Remembered from Easter
(May 9, 1941)

Suppose the world has all happened already
All this, already lived, only the sensations
Are just reaching us now,
After so many years
Like the light from the farthest star?

The Storm
    (May 15, 1941, during the blitz in Liverpool, England)

Helen must have felt like this,
When Troy was falling or about to fall,
Leaned on a parapet and seen a world
All wrapt in shadow flash with light
And disappear again. She must have wondered
Leaning there, if thoughts were only real
And she an image of an idea
Looking at a world of animate ideas
Or if the images alone were real
And thoughts only a mask to hide
Reality and wrap it in a cloud.

Helen must have felt like this
When once another world
       came to the same end.

Moon Is a Bent Feather
    (August 1, 1941)

The moon is a bent feather in the sky
And in the water where her spangled shadow lies
She is a pool of stars—of shining scales.
The soft hot wind is moving the leaves
And the grass stirs with night magic,
Your lips moving over me and slow speaking
And the dull soft music of insects—
I think the world will die before I forget tonight.

House Cleaning
    (October 16, 1941)

The past is locked away in notebooks
Scribbled on the margins of old histories.
Upon a battered plane geometry is Wagner.
Paris fell in Virgil—June long ago
And me in love with you, all on these pages.
I am burning old rubbish, old schoolbooks—
What more useless, what more the record of me?
What more to be forgotten, burned, and buried, as I will soon be.
All we have of the past is these
And the faint pulse under our wrists.

Now It Is Come
> *(December 9, 1941, two days after Pearl Harbor was bombed)*

Now it is come we are as calm as we have never been
We drink our coffee with still hands
And with grave eyes ask what is trump
Or whose lead now and carefully repair our rouge.
And read the *Tribune* and Thomas Aquinas
With equal imperturbability.
Once we were shifted by the sound of words
By great black headlines, by the screaming boy.

Now we are calm as we were calm in Troy
We are as silly as we ever were
But now our silliness is bravery
We are so shallow that the dying of a world
Cannot break through our consciousness
Or are so deep that it cannot.

That which we never quite believed has happened
And we touch inanely hands that never reach
And like a wounded lion, the world
Lies down to die with dignity.

We are as calm as we were calm in Troy.

Pledge
      (June 21, 1942)

If, perchance, the world should fail us
If, perchance, it all were dream
Nothing can this undiscover
Or unreal make it seem.

This is real if naught were real
This is true if truth were lies
This I'd feel though world were melting
This should see, though blind my eyes.

So do not fear the world will fail us
what has been will yet remain.
If we wake and find the world gone,
we shall turn and dream again.

Once
        (February 2, 1943, four months before her marriage to Bob Morrison)

I remember the clear cold day we met
All ice and shining snow and sun dazzling but chill.
The trees black and lacy against the snow-hills
And the figures of people standing out clear on the landscape.
You, with your green changing eyes turning to look at me
As I stood on the hill. Neat patterned fields far below
And charcoal sketches of smoke from chimneys and ice-white breath of cows
In the real world far below, while the gods walked on hills.
That was the first time we saw each other. Later
In the evening, things were not so sharp;
Around the fire inside, warmth blurred the figures that were clear-cut on the hill
And all I remember is lying by a log fire,
Warm glow on red wool and seeing your eyes on me.
There was good singing that night. Sweet old songs
And "You Made Me Love You."
I remember I liked your voice when I heard it.

Then there were other times too. A black cold night
And our first date and strong coffee at the Hitching Post
And your changing green eyes on me again.
Other times too—the first night you kissed me
Lake waves beating upon rocks and wind high in trees
And red lights of factories reflected in the skies
And white blown clouds racing by before I lost sight.
Friendship and fun and kisses followed as the days changed....
The dunes bright yellow in the spring—caught in a net of leaves
Beautiful dunes and strong happy laughter.

Summer...warm and lush and weird
Heavy yellow moon lying in a pool of clouds
Close enough to touch the earth, close enough to smother me
Shapes passing in the dark beyond, two by two, always two by two.
And the swollen moon eclipsed and dark
And blood red and the horror of old mystery
Seems beautiful—and dangerous.

War, even the war is beautiful, because it is so expected.
This world could not exist if there were not the undertone of tragedy.

The black shape is always moving
Across the face of the bright moon.

The songs that are trite to us now
May make us weep sometime because they bring back
Days that were when everything was yet to be done
And the world lay far below us—
Still to be ventured.
"I don't want to walk without you, baby"…
"I left my heart at the stage-door canteen"…
"This is worth fighting for…"
We may even cry because we remember
That "Mr. Five by Five" made us smile once
And the "Strip Polka" will seem quaint and old-fashioned.

Maybe we'll remember then
The day we first met
On a hill, while the world lay below us
Painted with black trees on snow
Traced with the steaming breath of cows
And black wisps of smoke from chimneys
And hills beyond and a white road—
And the world—
   Still to be ventured.

Darling, if we come to nothing
Let's not forget that.
Let's not forget
We stood on top of the world once.

If There Were No More World
    (January 31, 1944)

If there were no more world
    We should still sit as we are now,
    Arm touching arm,
    Look out the window into nothingness
    And sigh contentedly
    As we do now;

    And in that never-never land,
    That is within ourselves,
    Should stand together, arms entwined,
    Gaze steadfastly
    At what had never been.

    Nothing should change
    Only the world be gone
    And entities exist as once
    We should be still together,
    Only our frame
    Dissolved.

Author Bio

Joan Wehlen Morrison (1922-2010) was born in Chicago to a Swedish immigrant father and a mother of Ukrainian-Jewish heritage. Poor and working class, Joan received a scholarship to study at the University of Chicago. A resident of Morristown, NJ, Joan was the co-author of *American Mosaic: The Immigrant Experience in the Words of Those Who Lived It* (1980), recognized as a *New York Times* Notable Book of the Year. Dramatic readings from the book have been performed on Ellis Island, at the Mark Taper Forum in Los Angeles, and in an "In Performance at the White House" program broadcast nationally on PBS. Her second book, *From Camelot to Kent State: The Sixties Experience in the Words of Those Who Lived It* (1987), became the basis for her popular course on the 1960s at the New School in New York City. Joan's wartime diaries have been published as *Home Front Girl: A Diary of Love, Literature, and Growing Up in Wartime America* (2013).

Editor Bio

Susan Signe Morrison, professor of medieval English literature at Texas State University, is the author of dozens of scholarly articles and four books on the Middle Ages: *Women Pilgrims in Late Medieval England: Private Piety as Public Performance; Excrement in the Late Middle Ages: Sacred Filth and Chaucer's Fecopoetics; The Literature of Waste: Material Ecopoetics and Ethical Matter;* and *A Medieval Woman's Companion: Women's Lives in the European Middle Ages*. Author of the novel *Grendel's Mother: The Saga of the Wyrd-Wife,* Susan edited Joan Wehlen Morrison's diaries as *Home Front Girl*. She lives in Austin, Texas.

www.ingramcontent.com/pod-product-compliance
Lightning Source LLC
LaVergne TN
LVHW041550070426
835507LV00011B/1030